PLAYING FOR ENGLAND

David Scott was born in 1947 in Cambridge. He was educated at Solihull School, and studied Theology at Durham and then at Cuddesdon College near Oxford. He spent two years as a curate in Harlow and then became School Chaplain at Haberdashers' Aske's School, Elstree, where he taught religious education. Since 1980 he has been vicar of Torpenhow and Allhallows in the Diocese of Carlisle.

In 1978 David Scott won the *Sunday Times*/BBC national poetry competition with his poem 'Kirkwall Auction Mart'. *A Quiet Gathering*, his first book of poems, was published by Bloodaxe Books in 1984, and won him the Geoffrey Faber Memorial Prize in 1986. His second collection, *Playing for England* (Bloodaxe Books, 1989), is a Poetry Book Society Recommendation. Both *A Quiet Gathering* and *Playing for England* are illustrated with drawings by Graham Arnold. A collection of poems for children, *How Does It Feel?* was published by Blackie in 1989.

David Scott has also written several plays for the National Youth Music Theatre with Jeremy James Taylor. These include *Captain Stirrick*, which was staged at the National Theatre's Cottesloe Theatre in 1981; *Bendigo Boswell*, which was commissioned by the BBC and screened in 1983. *Jack Spratt VC* was performed in the 1986 London International Opera Festival, and *Les Petits Rats* was performed at the Edinburgh International Festival and Sadlers Wells in 1988.

In 1986 BBC Television produced and showed *A Private Voice*, Mark Scrimshaw's documentary about David Scott.

He is married to Miggy, and has three children, Adam, Lucy and Jonathan.

Graham Arnold is a member of the Brotherhood of Ruralists.

Playing for England

DAVID SCOTT

with drawings by Graham Arnold

BLOODAXE BOOKS

ISBN: 1 85224 071 7

First published 1989 by
Bloodaxe Books Ltd,
P.O. Box 1SN,
Newcastle upon Tyne NE99 1SN.

Bloodaxe Books Ltd acknowledges
the financial assistance of Northern Arts.

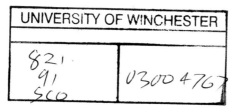
Typesetting by EMS Phototypesetting, Berwick upon Tweed.

Printed in Great Britain by
Baker Brothers (Litho Ltd), Pontefract, West Yorkshire.

For my father and mother

Acknowledgements

Acknowledgements are due to the editors of the following publications in which some of these poems first appeared: *The Franciscan, The Green Book, The Keswick Reminder, New Writing from the North* (MidNAG, 1988), *Owl, Poetry Book Society Anthology 1988-89* (PBS/Hutchinson, 1988), *Poetry Voice*, and *Poetry with an Edge* (Bloodaxe Books, 1988).

'Flower Rota' was commissioned by the Carlisle Cathedral Flower and Heritage Festival (1984). 'Castlerigg Songs' was set originally by the composer John Woolrich. 'Village Organist' was published in a series of Harlow Organ Club Newsletters. 'For Norman Nicholson' was published in *Between Comets* (Taxus Press, 1984). 'Just a Line' was written for the Geoffrey Holloway 70th Birthday Festschrift.

'The Church Boiler' was broadcast on *Poetry Now* (BBC Radio 3). 'Heart', 'Pulling Out Weeds' and 'Flower Rota' were broadcast in BBC Television's documentary, *A Private Voice*.

Contents

Flower Rota

This is my week for flowers.
It half says so on the damp notice in the porch.
(I had to borrow the pen from the Visitors' Book
and the ink ran out before my name.)
A few, who have let fall into their hearts
similar tragedies to mine, know why I chose this week
when flowers are hard to come by.
Each year I tell the season by a bowl of flowers,
whether things are late or soon, and predict
with those who visit here while I arrange,
the future course of summer.
They don't know for whom I struggle
to get this stalk through the chicken wire,
and it doesn't matter. When they are gone,
names half written in the Visitors' Book,
I'll have a moment when it's just
the flowers, the memory, and the sweet time it took.

Cross Canonby

The waves of the rigged field
beat against the ploughed sea.

Farmers and sailors: their headstones
akimber from persistent wind.

Rush light in the window, family Bible,
pend the docking of the clipper.

Tea, tobacco, turnips: the same face but
different boots share the year's saga.

Skiddaw House

The House was one of the loneliest dwelling-places in all the British Isles
HUGH WALPOLE

Left for us to assume what purpose
it once had other than shelter;
remote in the bowl of hills behind Skiddaw
deep in its own decay; the peace stuns,
the filth accumulates, the questions gnaw.
How did anyone manage? Did they feed
on the shifting view of mountain tops?
Why put the windows facing north-east?
Some say it was for the shoot,
for nights away from the Big House
to be near the butts. Others that
it was given to shepherds
for weeks at a time, and they survived
because they knew there was somewhere else
nearer the auction and the ale.
Yet what if once it had been a family
living there, taking silver water from the beck
and setting off for a day's walk
to Keswick or Bassenthwaite.
Growing up taught by the hills' silence;
reading the shifting mist; working out God's pattern
from this piece of it. The larch coppice
smoothed into shape by the wind.
The gate into the four rows of vegetables
now on one hinge.

Castlerigg Songs

I

Before dawn,
before chanting broke the wind's silence,
before shadows,
before the sheep's first tug at the grass
when the backs of the great beasts
resurrected in the light
there was the mystery.

II

Cleft fast in the stone's skin
is a lichen tuft. It is the air's
embroidery: silent, slow, patient, deft.

III

I throw up grass to see
which way the wind blows.
It is tugged all ways:
no shelter in any angle of the stones:
buttercup frantic in the wind:
wool holding tight to a blade of grass.

IV

There is to be one stone mightier than the rest:
a king of stones, from which all the land
can be seen and divided. This is the place.
Set it down here. Set others round it.
Make an order of stones
starting from the mighty stone.
Set it down for good.

V

No mark, no runes,
only the sheep's rubbing;
no illumination;
no face, no feature;
I mark a place
that is all.
I set against fuss
stone, air, earth,
being born, death.

Playing for England
(for Robert Hanvey)

He sat by the boot shop window
fettling the studs for Saturday's match,
his apron slashed almost to shreds.
As farm carts bounced back from the fields
he thought of the new schoolteacher,
and the match. The Match.
It kept coming back to that.

The lasts, the knife, and the needle
were set aside for the weekend
so he could scrummage with unaccustomed
other shoulders. He left the last shoe
to be mended, with the thread dangling.

Chosen to play for England
in the year of the General Strike
he shook the hand of George V
at Twickenham. His white strip engaging
the king's black overcoat and bowler.

Rose on the chest, buttons and collar;
full, pocketed shorts; bandage garters;
dubbin and embrocation.
The rest was himself:
solid, neckless Cumberland.

The match was the usual mixture
of dread and exultation, cracking of heads,
snotting out of one nostril.
He gum-shielded his half-time orange
and on his hunkers took in the tactics.
The scrum steamed as the light dwindled.

Feeding out the notched leather strap
for letting the window down of the last train
he was the only one to alight:
tasselled, velvet cap in the bag.

16

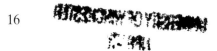

London was a single bird's song away.

They lost, but never mind.
There was the home ground
looking up to the mountains;
the schoolteacher encouraging
her African violets; and round about
the folks' shoes to make and mend.

A Line of Wordsworth's
(after Théophile Gautier)

Of all the Wordsworth I have read (the poet
On whom Byron expended so much venom),
The only line I have by heart is
'Spires whose silent finger points to heaven.'

I found it as an epigraph
To the first chapter of *Louisa*,
A Virgin's Lament, in a book of short stories
Called *The Dead Donkey* – if you please!

This line, fresh and holy, dropped
Into a volume of sweaty affairs, moved me
As if it were a wild flower, or a bird's feather
Floating into a dark cellar.

Since then, when words will not be summoned –
My Prospero disobeyed by Ariel –
On the blank sheet of paper I doodle spires,
their silent fingers pointing to heaven.

Skiddaw

A headscarf tied beneath her jaw,
the curtains of her eyes drawn
and drawn back, we talked about Skiddaw.
How from childhood she watched the dawn
rise behind it, and now propped on pillows
she could see it darken against the night.
Always it had been there and would be always
long after our eyes were tight shut.
Perhaps it is enough for one life,
one mountain. Given time
she would have photographed it
in all weathers: sheeting down, fine.
It was to do with time and eternity
like Hokusai's passion for Mount Fuji,
and his saying, 'If heaven had given me
five years more, I should have been a great painter.'

Stones on a Dorset Beach

Stirring invisible dust, bleached
through millenia, we crunch our way
across a *Shell Guide to Dorset* beach,
picking up stones. I choose this one,
Adam that one. He says his,
a piece of cloudy glass the shape of a heart
and two pure white stones
suitable for a sling or a still life
are not as good as mine.
Mine are door stops. Lucy's
are the rare mottled brown ones;
and for Jonathan there is a rule:
'only as many as you can carry'.
Surveyed by the fossil-locked cliff
our bent heads and occasional stoops
signal both the random and the fixed.
The cove-long waves repeat their off rhythm.
Dust whitens our shoes.

Monday

Washing the regimental off-white woollens
by the crab apple tree, they smelt the malt,
flicked a glance at embedded bottles,
imagined their hair floating like the weed.
Lathering was hard, then the bashing
on the stones; wring, wrench; unravel;
wring, wrench; and a moment's pang
for the skin beneath the scarlet.
Unaware that the cholera rilled
along the stream; under their reddening knuckles
it filled the buckets all the way to the mill.

A Prayer on the North Side

The mowers can't get easily
over established tufts.

So the brambles tie up the parcels
of this ramshackle park.

While everyone files out of the south
I go to the north side to be soothed

by its lack of attention. The tall
unclipped yews wave a high hello.

Reading Party

Someone had a house by Windermere.
It was good air for a reading party.
So up they came: soft leather bags
containing delicacies, pushed down
between the clerical socks and the Tracts,
to compensate for the local fare.
In the earnest silence of the night
they surprised each other on the stairs,
and in the library searched for something
the fresh air did not seem to give them.
The mountains were not enough. They were
homesick for a Comper baldachino
to narrow down the glory. It took a week
for them to assume a doctrine of creation;
longer still to skim a pebble on the lake.

Locking the Church

It takes two hands to turn the key
of the church door, and on its stiffest days
needs a piece of iron to work it like a capstan.
I know the key's weight in the hand
the day begins and ends with it.
Tonight the sky is wide open
and locking the church is a walk
between the yews and a field of stars.
The moon is the one I have known
on those first nights away from home.
It dodges behind the bellcote
and then appears as punched putty or a coin.
The key has a nail for the night
behind the snecked front door.
Carrying a tray of waters up to bed
I halt a careful tread to squint
through curtains not quite met
at the church, the moon, and the silver light
cast on the upturned breasts of the parish dead
locked out for the night.

Excerpts from the Passion
Translations of George Herbert's Latin poems

1   ***On the Sweating***

Where do you run to, sweat?
Christ does not know, nor his veins.
Does it not please you to stay in that
body of all bodies? If not,
no other body will please you, I can vouch for that;
unless it's mine you're after,
the least worthy, to make you most worthy,
by my rescue.

2   ***On the Spitting and Railing***

Savages, on the holy face, right side
which to look on is to live
you spit; and on the turned side
as fresh as the water of life, you spit
and swear. Beware
lest the whole fig tree race, right cheek
left cheek, be cursed. Good people of the living water
prepare cups, flagons, buckets,
the Aqueduct is yours.

3   ***On the Buffeting***

My mother made a poultice
for chest colds; bashed it into a bread shape
with the heel of her hands.
So, remedy for all mankind
thou was spun round blind,
and beaten before, on top, behind.

4 *On the Whipping*

Christ, hope of the whipped, victor of the world
when crimes multiply, and my punishment draws near
may your more gentle whip, the shadow of your whip, suffice.
Tender minds duplicate blows for themselves.
Soft hearts are their own whips.

5 *On the Nails*

What sort wast thou
but a better nature
that took a less from ours
and was nailed to the cross.
Now thou art mine. I have thee.
The shepherd caught by the
nails and wood as if by his own scythe.

Churchyard under Snow

The newer headstones tense against the cold
having no moss to befriend the snow;
and footsteps to them are specific, directed
not for idle search, but to a particular bolster of earth.
Year long widowers right a tipped vase
and shake the Christmas wreath back into greenness.
A thrush cascades snow off a bouncing
high branch and offers its clear song
over the uniform white ground.
The cold makes it so much worse,
indiscriminate in its disregard
for the memory of this one's summer dress
and the angle of that one's cap over his shrewd brow.
We used to hurry them inside from the cutting wind:
now, from that unimaginable weathering
we can only trust their souls do well to fly.

The Surplice

To think so many battles have been fought
over this four and a half yard circumference
of white linen. Not just by those who ironed it
up to the difficult tucks beneath the yoke
but by Divines wrangling over rubrics.
For me it is my only finery, by law
decent and comely; a vestry friend
put on often in dread; given away
to old deft fingers to mend.
I have seen them hanging in as many ways
as there have been voices chanting in them:
immaculate in hanging wardrobes; or worn
with the peg mark still obtruding;
or chucked on the back seat of the car
with the purple stole and the shopping.
We have put these garments on for centuries.
They persist. We wither and crease inside them.

A Walk with St Teresa of Avila

We chose the low cliffs first, and then
to come back along the beach into the falling sun.
It was November and there was no wind, just
a bluish, evening mist.
She spoke of arrows wounding her heart, and stripping
everything away that came between her and Christ.
The breakwaters were bleached and purified
by a century of salt pounding tide.
The sun, a huge and softened red, reigned
above dark roofs and the steeple
as the lights came on beneath.
I think she didn't notice it was the eighteenth green
we finished up on; some late players were judging
the camber and then missing. In the clubhouse
by the light of table lamps, I saw the ladies
sorting cards out on the baize. Charitably,
Saint Teresa said that everyone is a bunch
of dried rosemary, and I could see the longing in her eyes
for more of the wounds of love and for the darts
that score the heart.

Hopkins Enters the Roman Catholic Church

Dressed mainly in black and with hair
shading the upper lip,
he took the railway from Oxford
to Birmingham; fingernails, collar, notebook
all much grubbier than we would suppose.
The journey was an absolute offering
in the dark. The tunnels confirmed this.
The shattering thunder of iron
recalled the opposition to his choice:
Father, Mother, Canon Liddon –
'Do have the courage to stop, even now.'
In his notebook, the design
for a decanter stopper. Looking at the oaks
in the parks he wondered how he would get
to the Oratory on the Hagley Road.
For comfort he thought that being alone
might double charge his spirit, but good,
they were expecting him, and yes,
he was Mr Hopkins and this was
all he had brought. They arrived in the dark,
and the leaves blown into the hall of the house
scratched on the chequered floor
as far as Doctor Newman's room.

Atkinson of Danby

It seemed essential for him to stay put
resisting all offers of preferment
or a move nearer the shops at Scarborough.
He found it difficult at first, missing
the softness of the Essex marshes,
and coping with a sour and empty church;
but as the Lents and Trinitys came round
for the fortieth time, he no longer searched
for novelty beyond the parish bounds.
It was largely the Yorkshire turn of phrase
that held him tightly to his moorland place
listening, writing it down for the Glossary.
He dug words out, like earth chucked
shoulder high from a deepening grave.
The shards and bones of the old talk,
as well as a few faithful souls, were saved.

Richard Watson Dixon
(1833-1900)

Left-handed you wrote into your ink
incorporating references
to tenth century monks
and the British garden birds.
Scanning the long poems
for anything left behind by the critics
I was hoping for a gem
fired in the rectory in the room
overlooking the tennis court.
I sometimes wonder if the poems
had been more a matter of life or death
rather than an adjunct to
your History of the Church of England
there might have been a masterpiece
with lines that soldiers called to mind
and girls took through to lonely womanhood.
Hubris was your talent,
and sadness,
and putting poems, it seems,
where they are hard
but not impossible
to find.

Village Organist

1 *Short Prelude*

Grace was sung to Melcombe
(New Every Morning is the Love)
while the polish and turnips
mulched to an indelible memory
for the pianist. She was ten.
Her legs dangled above the pedals.
It was the vicar's wife took notice
knowing that Melcombe would do
for almost any hymn, and asked
if Mary Ann could be encouraged
to play a hymn in church.
There were always boys to blow the organ
but rarely girls to play it.
So this was a discovery
unheard of from the village.

2 *Introductory Voluntary*

The vicar led her to the organ
as if to some returning aunt
she had never met before. It stood there
straight-backed with its decorated pipes,
ivory keys, and knobs –
'Oh! the stops, don't worry about those
just pull them all out' –
the high up importance of the seat
with its piece of Turkey carpet cushion.

'Try Melcombe,' said the vicar, 'I'll pump for you
this once.' The pumping was vigorous,
distracting, his white shirt
flapping from behind his stock.
In two sharps were blown
the first few notes of a lifetime's playing.
From then on, the weekly list of hymns
would come before her, numbers

as resonant as the words. With each new vicar
she gauged the announcement of the hymn:
some brisk, some devotional, some didactic;
as various as the boys who came
to pump for her, the vicar's lads
who, when the blower went electric,
slipped away onto the tractor seats
careless of Sunday.

3   *Funeral March*

> *'It was proposed that the organist be given £2*
> *a year advance in salary – on the understanding*
> *that she would play at funerals when desired.'*

She would play them in and play them out
and for bride as well as coffin
she would squint through her curtain screen
hat bobbing back and forth
to catch the vicar's sign or his voice
'I am the resurrection and the life...'
Between The Lord's My Shepherd
and Abide With Me she browsed among
the clothy pages of her annotated hymn book:
the vicar's favourite; verses to omit
from the long processional hymns;
alternative tunes borrowed from the chapel.
Her shoe heels safe
behind the cross-bar of the stool.

4   *Second Tune*

> *'The organist of a parish church, although appointed*
> *and paid by the vestry, is guilty of an ecclesiastical*
> *offence if he plays on the organ during Divine service*
> *contrary to the directions of the incumbent.'*

Not long before she retired for the first time,
there was the terrible day of the note. That week
the vicar decided on the second tune
for a familiar hymn. The choirmistress was informed

but she did not like it. The practices were hard work.
The second tune did not flow like the first one.

Come the day of the first time to sing the new tune,
right in the middle of the service, a note came
from the choirmistress to the organist –
'Play the old tune.'
The organist went cold. The open diapason bass
thrummed all through her, gonging
in her empty stomach. She loved the vicar.
She was terrified of the choirmistress.

The hymn was announced,
and she would always remember this,
she would date her life before and after it,
she played the new tune. Why should pain
like this get even into the chancel?

The vestry was somewhere she never went,
but this day, the day of the terrible note,
she went into its strange, curtained
unfamiliarity and cried, caught between two wills.
The vicar, versed in law and handkerchiefs,
helped her to wipe the tears, and later,
to face the choirmistress from whom
because of the distance to the branch-line
there was no immediate escape.

5   *Chanting the Proper Psalms*

The Cathedral Psalter had such a dark cover
that she often mislaid it in the gloom.
The word "cathedral" gave her aspirations
which she transposed for the meagre congregation:
two of whom were deaf; one always without her glasses;
and the one who found the twenty third morning
in time to catch the 'Glory be to the Father'.
The words in her book took on a new intensity
with their upright strokes marking off
the syllables, and there were asterisks

which, coming at the end of a long line
when they could sing no more without exploding,
allowed them breath. What the references
to Leviathan or the water pipes meant
was another matter. Winter's meaning
seeped into summer's stone; meaning
was there when they needed it,
brought on by the repetition of the days.

6   *Finale*

In the end it got too much for her, as one finger
after another went permanently cream.
She was waking at four to play at nine.
In her mind her last service would have been the finest
with all her favourite tunes; instead,
it was a new invention for Christmas
with songs the children were meant to know
with the words stuck up on the walls.
The icy wind seemed against her both ways
as she went to get her pension. Church
was the last straw. After the service
as her bandaged ankle passed the garage
they suggested she came in and sat down.
It seemed there were no tunes left in her,
and to all who stopped for petrol, it was declared
that she was ill, and the unspoken verdict was
that, as far as the organ was concerned, that was it.
As for the hymn books and music, well,
they could stay where they were
with the note book, her glasses, and her pencil.

Brother Douglas Looks After the Bees

The hives were somewhere near the apple trees,
(the Standard W. Broughton Carr Hive)
white, with room for the bees to live,
room to expand, and room to thrive.
He would set off with three essentials:
cat, garden fork, boater with veil,
looking like something from the Army and Navy Stores
by way of Lady Ottoline Morrell.
The way to the bees was through central Italy.
Dorset was Umbria: the one burnt, with ilex trees,
the other lush after it had poured;
one with ox and cart, the other with a worn-out Ford.
When the sun of the canticle did not shine
he did his best with the whitewash,
the naming of the houses (Juniper, Clare), Mowbrays'
reproductions, and costumes for the Housman plays.
His gloveless manipulation of the bees
satisfied an instinct in him which was Franciscan,
energy controlled by stillness,
England and Italy combining
in the laughter and the ceaseless gardening.
It was a problem of language too.
Italian vowels reduced to the tight precision
of a Saxon consonant: from Giacomo to James
a pulling in of the reins; from *sole* to sun
to do with the magic of just catching it.
On the morning of the photograph
the sun caught one lens of his spectacles;
the hives; and later in the day
escaped between beeches all the way to Dorchester Market,
onto jars of honey clanking in the back.

The Sunday School Cupboard

It has all become unusable,
another generation's way of doing things,
and yet there is no throwing it out.
I would save them from others' dustbins:
the wall pictures wrapped in a great bundle
unrolled reveal the angels ascending
and descending on a crumpled ladder.
The felt-backed shepherds and the stamp books
with rusty staples should have gone long ago.
All of Advent Sunday's stamps
are stuck together in a great wodge.
A book for the teacher written for
two hundred children who could sit still.
The vital pegs for the blackboard,
the light wooden cross, the wrap over hymns,
the prayer cards passe-partouted,
the cigar-box carpenter's bench,
which has its shavings still inside
breathing a devotion to the geography
of the Holy Land, recall the ghosts of spinsters
devoted to the rector. While the parents
slept off their week's work and Sunday lunch
this teacher made her register a work of art
and for the children caused the heat to shimmer
over the road from Jerusalem to Jericho.

The Marquis of Ripon Purchases
the Convent of San Damiano

Up a steep hill and out of town,
looked after by a shuffling, aproned verger
doubling as housekeeper to the priest
was Ripon's Roman Catholic Church,
St Wilfred's; where Lord Ripon lit the first
eager candles of his conversion.
Was it there the idea came to him
to buy back San Damiano's from the State,
at a time when places such as those
were realising very low prices?
He thought of all the place had meant to him
(cicadas, cypress, thyme,
the ancient conjunction of wood and stone,
the lack of any compulsion to respond)
when he had visited there with his friend
and water-colourist, W. B. Richmond.
The Count of Cavour would have knocked it down,
used the benches for levering gun-carriages
out of the mud in his fight against the Austrians,
and stolen the brittle, silver hair,
probably not St Clare's, and used it
for stuffing King Victor Emmanuel's footstool.
But there, Francis heard the crucifix speak,
and Clare wrote letters to the Blessed Agnes of Prague
signing herself 'useless handmaid'.
For these and other reasons, Lord Ripon paid
all those noughts of lires
arguing over the exchange of currency
and mistranslations, so that the nuns
could filter back under no pressure to be useful.
San Damiano's, the place where Francis wrote
Il Cantico di Frate Sole, under its Yorkshire landlord
was returned to an acre of grace.

The Closure of the Cold Research Institute

Was it at Berkhamsted or Tring?
Well, anyway, it's just packed in.
Boffins' heads like Friedrich Nietzsche's
are seen emerging from the Chiltern beeches.
Olitsky and Macartney with files untold
have failed to trap the common cold.
We've got the hang of the other species,
we can tell which are the foreign cheeses.
Most common things we understand:
sparrows, cormorants, Prayers, and land,
but colds defy the common wit.
You get them, and that's it.
So that's it too for volunteers
and bottles labelled over many years;
tons of bumph and Government Issue
pulped into rolls of lime green tissue.
Still the nation's noses run
impervious to tots of rum.
The mother's eagerness to wipe
is countered by the child's swipe.
The dreadful sweat of boardroom meetings,
the midnight shakes, the fitful sleeping,
days off school, off work, off life,
the 'don't come near me's' of the wife,
all these presumes a fierce defiance
of man's experimental science.
We cannot check the flow of phlegm
or staunch the faulting speaker's 'hem'.
So if there are no more suggestions,
we'll have to be content with questions:
Which of the primates had it first?
Which of the Royal's had it worst?
If God intended it for man
what exactly was his plan?

The Church Boiler

Robert W. Pitt Ltd. Milburn House (B Floor), Newcastle-on-Tyne.
For one new six Section Water Circulating Boiler supplied
and fitted in position to your satisfaction. Removing
old Boiler and connecting up to your existing pipes as
arranged – £41-10
26th November, 1932

1st August, 1932

Dear Mr Pitt, I'm told
it's possible you have a better system
of heating to offer to a poor parish
than the old one we have, which is furred up
and has poor circulation, so that some radiators
are starved of heat. The complaints
are justified. Something must be done,
of course it must, and it is my
responsibility: not only preaching sermons
but also keeping the people warm.

10th September, 1932

I'm so pleased that you can help. Newcastle
seems a long way from Cumberland:
you and your man will spend the night, I hope,
and over here we have a man who helps.
We are so dependent on the goodwill
of the sexton. He does his best:
coming every Saturday night with his torch,
he shovels the coke, lights the boiler,
and carts away the ash. I can hear it
from the Vicarage but leave him to it
hoping he keeps a straight path to the ash-pit.
He will do anything for you except come to church.

15th September, 1932

You say the new boiler will be larger
and displace the coke. That will mean a new
coke pile and a lean-to for it. More work for the sexton;
more requests for kindness. How difficult I find that!
Bob will do it, but his pace
will signify that it's a favour. I'd do it myself
but then he'd say it was his job.

12th October, 1932

I don't understand the significance
of an increase of 20,000 Thermal Units.
All I know is what a difference it makes
to be warm, and how it will cost
more than we can think of or can easily manage to pay.
But this must be the story everywhere,
and a Sale will go a long way to meet the cost.
So whenever you and your man can come
we shall be pleased to see you. I'll ask the sexton
if he can help, when he's not busy at the Garage.

7th November, 1932

When you left last Monday
and we thought everything was fine
one of the small pipes on the boiler
had commenced to leak. There's always
something, isn't there. Could you get a new fitting
sent through with your man?
We would like to light up the boiler for the service
on the Twenty Third Sunday after Trinity.
For the last few Sundays
it's been cold here, but not severe.
How dependent we are in our Church for warmth.
We cater largely for the old.

23rd November, 1932

I'm sorry to trouble you again
but the boiler now seems to be overheating.
I know you'll understand if I say that a service
held under threat of an explosion is not conducive
to the rest and quietness advocated by the Evening Collect.
It makes everyone nervous. The sexton
says that it's probably easy to control
but he would value your opinion.

13th December, 1932

We have taken note of your suggestion
and installed, at least the sexton has,
a pipe which can take the overflow of boiling water.
That is a relief. Such a simple thing
needing just 'a little common reason' as you say.
We have put a thermometer by the lectern
so every time I read the lesson I think
of your common reason and the fount
of heavenly wisdom. The Sale helped raise the funds,
and we have pleasure in settling your account.

Whit Monday

We parked between what was left of the great forest
and the area set aside for the sheepdog trials,
where Elliots and Frasers in battered suits
whistled their dogs into the utmost stealth.
Morris men, arms and legs going both ways,
trod the deep vat of courtyard chippings
while the Regimental Band puffed among the topiary
waiting for the capering with handkerchiefs to end.
The Dean popped up now and then from counting the cars.
It was far too cold to lounge about, and some,
still shaky from a dose of winter 'flu
edged their way through the vintage cars
to their own securer model with its rug and tissues.
A helicopter growled at the retreating, long grass.
The voice from the by-election speakers was a help
but the wind blew it out of range
as one hand struggled with the cornets
and the other fished under the plastic mac for change.
Trodden grass gave off its own smell.
We were about the last to leave. The emptying park
revealed the bales of straw by the marquee.
The car was lighter by a picnic; heavier
by a garden plant, bought just to show we'd been.
We took a fresh grass route out: the so-called grown-ups
in the front, and strapped into the back,
the emperor and empress of ice cream.

Maths Master

Cambridge was his only real time away
when the Senior wranglership gave vent
to his one brief exclamation of joy.
At other times it was shy, pointed comments
humphed out of an anxiety to keep all angles
perfect. On the full-sized billiard table it went
white to red, red off the cushion, and red pocketed;
upstairs the gramophone speakers and chair arranged
for the maximum stereo effect; and on holiday
climbing Scafell or Snowdon, unencumbered,
he strove to make the route isosceles.
Boyhood, manhood, old age spent
in the same school, round the same paths.
Theorems, chalk, marks: a celibate for Maths.
Any deviation from the rule he could not bear.
When errors occurred that ought not to have done
in his own handling of things, like adding up,
he slipped by night and without a word
to anyone, into Archimedes', by then cold water.

For Norman Nicholson

It was a long way round from
Ulverston on the road to Millom.
We passed the low sands and the gulls
and the first outcrop of the hills
until at 'the west of the west'
– his phrase – we reached a film set
of the 1930s, stage and props.
You could tread on a whole row of shops
and chapels. So many corners to lean against.
So much shoring up of the corrugated fence.
That must be the house
with its old shop window doused,
where you can sit in the back
and join in the front street crack.
Over the roofs, Black Combe,
and yonder the silent doom
of Windscale. All this has been set
down in words, from the Good Friday sonnet
of the first wartime anthology
to the dazzle of the Easter Sunday sea.

Childhood Triptych

I
Stammering his way out of
the priesthood,
perpetual deacon
never at the altar
more under the black cloth
left hand waving out messages
to stay still
stay still, my little girl,
'that's beautiful'.

II
So black at one moment
except for the wide eyes
beneath the cap
above the knotted scarf
saying 'why, o why'.
And then all white
and wings and fronds
of drifting weed in the river
swimming naked over the black deep.

III
Some inevitable confusion
between the window wide open
to the night and the curtains blowing
and the sail on my boat
flapping, adrift on the pond.
Between a boy and a girl
looking out in wonder
at a painted sky, and
wondering myself how grandma
could be so foolish as to let go
the string as she launched my boat.
So that when I see the one
I see the other, and when I see the other
I see the one: park and play,
statue and lost boat.

Just a line
(for Geoffrey Holloway)

It happened
having just cracked the spine
that my eye
and mind found the perfect
converting line.

Before was never
the same as after.
The line will go with me
to the grave, perhaps
see me through it.

It was something to do with
a swimming pool
and the feeling of trust
between swimmer
and water, father
and daughter.

I had felt it
and you had said it,

poet.

Packers

When it was Mr Lawrence
and Mr Hall, in the days
of tea chests and dust sheets,
and labels tied with coarse, hair string
you just had to ask and they would know
which hold and for how long.
After all, these suits
flat arms folded in and letters bundled
and the stones and the driftwood
packed within the packing
were part of you, were you.
They were things that you would miss.

Mr Lawrence and Mr Hall
appreciated this.

Hamada

O for just the deft
touch of a Hamada
in my teaching –
bold, thick strokes
fearless of mistake.
He used to walk along
a line of pots, a pupil
holding the paint,
asperging them.
Nothing could go wrong.
With every pot he hit the mark.
The merest flick: a song.

Daffodils

In winter when I pass that orchard
I forget what it can be like. Dashing
to the library, dentist, or garage
there seems no time to remember.
The orchard is just over a hedge, and has four
or five apple trees: a place to peg out washing,
let chickens roam, tie a swing. Pleasing
but not enough to stop me in my tracks.
My neighbour who cycles that way every day
will know what I mean when I say,
April is different. All winter
clenched in frost or sogged in rain
they hide. Today I stop the car,
no errand too important for honouring,
with some awkward parking, the sight in sun and wind
of this green and yellow jamboree of daffodils.

Pulling Out Weeds

Whoever hath a mind to weed will never want work

Buttercup
It accepts a firm grip at the waist
and a shake of its skirt of root
to free it from the loosened soil.
It comes without complaining, hands up.
Its languishing butter heads
slopping out of the wheelbarrow.

Forget-me-not
At the end of May,
from this skirt of washed blue
under the apple trees
as much as on a market day
we'll take a few, making an alleyway
for boots and bare knees.

Ground elder
Preferring shale and bits of glass
to bed in and flourish, linked
in a mafia of underground handshakes,
only gentle handling will reveal the connections
and then it will come out whole
like a lifted jigsaw.

Dandelion
Leave them as a field of brittle haloes
until the last second blows away
and then dig deep for its carrot root.
The root is tough as the stalk is brittle.
To crack the naked hollow stalk in idler days
meant a slippery rub and the bitterest spittle.

Daisy
The soil's brooch. It will come off
from behind, by teasing its clasping thin roots
away from the mud; but used to a tight lawn
it will not always come clean.

Cow Parsley
You can tell by the crown of lace and the tall walk
that this is her wedding day.
It takes two hands in a tug-of-war
to lift her from her primacy.
She knows where her strength lies
and she is holding on to it.

Nettle
Some can take them by the hand, the old gardeners.
Others pick them for their goodness.
I tackle them low
where their ragged turkey necks of stalk
have no leaves, no chance of mottling the skin,
no need for spit and docks.

The Wild Boar

The scratchable hide crashing the bracken,
snuffling for roots in the vile weather,
racing from the spear. This was the beast
it was the legionary's duty to carve
on his section of the wall. A cognisance.
He imagined the turning spit, the singeing beard,
the forced apple smile, the thing bedecked.
More used to lettering altars, he had trouble
with the knees, getting the legs right,
its height from the ground,
the raised eyebrow, the twitching muzzle.
He didn't want anyone to see it
but duty...and it was a change from numerals
and it was good...and it had made him look.

(The wild boar was the emblem of the Twentieth Legion)

Berkeley

There is a table in my study.
I see and feel it. It contains my pen,
paper, envelopes, and note books,
and if I wasn't there, but visiting
in the parish, it would happily
content itself with being, for a while.
Whether anything perceives it
in my absence, God or some spirit,
casting a curious glance at rosary,
crucifix, photograph of former vicar,
is a mystery. I don't really need
that idea for the desk still to be there
when I return. It props my arm, paper,
pen, allowing me to write a sermon
on how all things hold their own by leaning
on something infinitely greater.

Heart

I thought of other significant hearts:
Christ's, which in the Greek
would throw itself out;
Shelley's saved from fire and water
brought back to Bournemouth.
Now this child's. The doctor's hand
went far either side of it.
The pink tubes of the stethoscope
divined an unfamiliar sluicing.
Something in nature was too tight.
Something in Greek had gone wrong,
and although it made the old phrases
new – 'take heart', 'with all my heart'
for three days we put them aside
until the valve, tough as tripe, came right.

East

The first tug at the straw in the heck,
crisp mud, breath as smoke, the last
of the stock left out,
as the light breaks behind Skiddaw.
To paint it – the gentlest wash in the paint-box
and one hair of crimson.
It will not get much colder than this.
I know it is only us diving slow motion
round the sun, but since stories began
the sun has done the rising,
this month the palest.
Mattins is walking round the church
chanting, 'Dayspring.
Another beginning.'

South

We always pack to go south,
compressing what we are,
letting other things have a go at us for a while:
fruit, bays of warm sand,
fishing boats, light thin as muslin.
South is always a summer journey,
the annual pilgrimage, jostling.
Is that where the birds are off to
flying in shifting formation over Brown Moor?
A royal progress
leaving us to get on with winter?

North

We do up all our buttons against the wind,
walking on hidden paths beside fields
of long shadow. The lichen
bruises the stone walls.
What the wind can't shift
is here to stay.
We learn the earth's slow lessons,
are cautious of angels,
make sure the doors shut.

West

West is the end of the day
when the spade and the fork are
put in the barrow and wheeled away.
Overalls are dumped in the wash
and the table is ready.
Grace is warmth, light, peace.
Beyond the garden wall
in the glebe, the bullock
gives its last bellow and with
a gentle rearrangement of limbs
collapses front legs first
onto the frosted earth
waiting for the light from the east
and the cracking of the ice
to quench its thirst.